sinfully
beat
poems

by
elliot m rubin

ISBN paperback 979-8-9922464-1-4
EPub 979-8-9922464-2-1

Library of Congress Control Number: 2025903407

Published 2025
Monroe Township, N.J.

Dedication

To my grandchildren
Shane, Isabelle, Jonathan, Carter,
Alexandra, Melanie, Mollie, and Madison

In memory of my father

Herman S. Rubin
who wrote poetry, prayers and letters all his life

Preface

I believe poetry is to be read and understood by all, and it needs to be written, for the most part, in plain language for everyone's enjoyment.

Too often, poets write in-depth, penetrating poems where you need to be well-read and/or versed in literary minutia to appreciate the poetry, not this book or any of my writings. I try to write so everyone can enjoy a few moments of intellectual satisfaction without consulting a dictionary or encyclopedia all the time.

Disclaimer

This book of poetry is not intended to be read by prudes, political book-banning conservatives, and/or sexually inhibited and repressed small-minded dolts.

What is Progressive Beat Poetry

Progressive beat poetry is a type of poetry that goes against the usual rules and traditions. It talks about social, political, and cultural issues to make people more aware and push for change. Here are some key points about progressive poetry:

- **Questioning the Norms**: Progressive beat poets often challenge and question the main social, political, and cultural ideas. They dive into complex topics like race, gender, and power.
- **Voices and Inclusion**: This poetry style aims to give a voice to those who are often ignored. It highlights stories and experiences that don't usually get attention.
- **Thinking and Talking**: Progressive beat poetry makes readers think about bigger societal issues and encourages meaningful conversations. It aims to start discussions and inspire actions towards social justice.
- **Breaking the Mold**: Progressive poets often play with form and structure, moving away from traditional styles to better express their messages.

Progressive beat poetry seeks to break free from traditional poetic conventions and push the boundaries of language, space-as-art, and expression.

Table of Contents

PARIS MEMORY 9

A GRAVE 10

EMMA 11

BORING POETRY 12

CORNER BAR DOWN THE STREET 13

MAGGIE SUBMITTED TO JUNIPER LITERARY JOURNAL 14

ENDINGS... 15

TOOTHPICKS 16

A POET'S LIFE SUBMITTED TO JUNIPER LITERARY JOURNAL 17

HE FOUND HIMSELF IN PARADISE 18

KING JAMES 19

PRETTY LITTLE GIRL 20

42ND STREET AND BROADWAY 21

WHALES ARE BIG MAMMALS 1963 22

MEMORY 23

POETIC BLUEPRINT FOR INSURRECTION 24

JERSEY PINE BARRENS 25

ENCHANTED DANCERS 26

SIXTY YEARS LATER 27

CHAOS IN THEIR LIVES 28

MAYBE, SOMEDAY 29

WAITING 30

WESTERN COWBOY MELODY 31

THE DAHMER CAT 32

FLOWERS 33

KLUB KISSES 34

SMOKE'N WITH WILLIE NELSON 35

WAR ZONE 36

ALL GROWN UP 37

I'LL LIVE WITH IT... 38

NEW ENGLAND COUNTRY STORE 39

I LONG TO BE BACK.. 40

UNFOLDED FUTURE.. 41

BA HUMBUG... 42

RETIREMENT... 43

CONFESSIONAL 44

FORLORN 45

WHEN A POET DIES.. 46

LUST 47

HOSPITAL EMERGENCY ROOM 48

SENIOR HOUSING DEVELOPMENT MAGIC SHOW 49

BALLOONS 50

ALMOST 51

FOREVER NEXT 52

POISON IVY 53

INFORMATION SCIENCE HYPOTHESES..................................... 54

ORANGE TABBY 55

WINDOWS.. 56

HOW DO YOU SAY GOODBYE 57

LOUISA OF EAST 8TH STREET, OFF 2ND AVENUE, N.Y.C. 58

WISDOM OF KING SOLOMON.. 59

NERDY, DIRTY, AND FLIRTY GIRLS 60

CRUEL SUMMER 61

OBSERVATIONS.. 62

WINTER 63

EMOTIONS... 64

SUMMER STORM 65

JANUARY STORM.. 66

FLORIST SHOP.. 67

EAST 21 STREET MEMORY 68

JOB JUSTIFICATION... 69

FREEDOM 70

REFLECTIONS OF AN OLD MAN 71

AGOG 72

ON A CITY STREET... 73

IF WE EVER MEET 74

AS AN OLD MAN 75

UNSEEN AND UNNOTICED... 76

SANCTUARY SECLUSION AND QUIETUDE 77

NEVER-ENDING LOVE 78

HER HEART PIERCED 79

RUBINO RISTORANTE CUCINA ITALIANO 80

WHY 81

PUSHERS, PIMPS, PROSTITUTES.. 82

BONES 83

LATE NIGHT MEETING 84

NOBODY NOTICES NINA 85

COSTCO.. 86

BLACK 87

BRILL BUILDING 1966 88

AN ARRANGEMENT..89

MAYBE A LETTER FROM LORD BYRON.....................................90

LOVE IS IN THE ARENA...91

SIMPLE JOY...92

MAGICAL KISS..93

STRONG TREES..94

ENOUGH..95

MY KISSES...96

BROKEN DREAM...97

LOLLIPOP GIRLS..98

RELATIONSHIP...99

ALMOST...100

LOVE QUESTION...101

BACKSTABBED..102

HELPLESSNESS...103

STAMPS...104

ROSALINE..105

A GIRL CALLED SPARKLE..106

PLAY THE APOLLO IN HARLEM...107

DISSECTION OF THE REPUBLICAN POLITICAL PARTY............108

WHISPERS..109

TRANS OCEAN FLIGHT..110

SPANISH FLU..111

LOTTERY..112

TWO ARE TOO MANY..113

HOSPITAL...114

TO CREATE A POEM..115

paris memory

submitted to Chewers for June 2024 edition

one night in paris years ago
on a worn-down, cobblestone narrow street
bright moonlight shines
as music flows from a concertina
near a corner's busy bistro
a small monkey
dances with a tin cup
while couples walk past arm in arm
and whisper lovings to each other

parisian born emily,
with her worn wool blue beret
tilted on short, scraggly brown hair,
holds my arm as we listen
while our summer romance
flowers in bloom and
tomorrow, my flight home awaits

i knew then
it was a memory to be cherished
as my scholarship expired, and
i lacked funds to return

our kiss that night was our last
over too soon, yet still lives
forty years later, at night
when i sit alone in my study
i always wonder,
what if i had missed the plane

a grave

they dig it
deep down
six feet
deep down
it's a law
diggers must obey
it has to go
deep down
dirt's piled high
shovels stand straight
as they wait
for finished final services

then diggers reverse
to fill it in
leave a small mound
wet with tears
while a tiny tin temporary marker
placed in a field of grass
pockmarked with brass plates
where field mice
dig deep down
as unacknowledged pets
next to the deceased

after a few dates
she wants marriage –
one night,
he starts a breakup talk
she needs a moment alone
cries and runs to her bedroom
he waits on the sofa
 twenty minutes later
   antsy
 thirty minutes later
  callout
 no answer
   gently knock on the door
 no answer
   slowly opens it
bloodstreams snake slowly on slit wrists
pools on pink and blue mini-floral sheets
try to stem with towels
empty barbiturate bottle on the floor –
in the emergency room
her estranged mother arrives
to shame her for mental illness
emma lies silent
unable to respond
while he sits quietly next to her body –
they only dated for a short time;
her intensity in life, he had to deal with
for years after

boring poetry
submitted to Seven Story Hotel, an online journal May 2024

how many:
    sunsets do you need to write about
    or the many trees that capture stanzas, sonnets
    flowers and green grassy fields
they're all pleasant

stop it already!

write about the unspoken and unseen
a wicked world where witches and bitches live
i want to read about the unseemly and godless
who make life interesting   and titillating
the bible-thumping two-faced hypocrites
who bring my blood to a boil
while they poison the good earth's soil
as they pontificate and procreate in sin
behind shuttered doors
                 out of sight
yet kneel in church as good, upright people
while they wallow in the lower levels of morality

write about them
at least they're interesting

corner bar down the street submitted to Juniper Literary Journal

every day, barstools
are filled with people
who come for cigarettes and whisky
while older bar broads sit, flit, flirt, and smile,
then get closer   talk in whispers   as they hope
to find a warm body for the night, nothing more —
while outside, the bitter winter wind chills   and
new lovers' arms intertwine while they huddle
in coats and jackets as they dash to a warm place
somewhere
        doesn't matter where
as long as you don't muss her hair
to have a one-night marriage
without long-term consequences
or contact numbers exchanged
only to meet again soon
at the corner bar down the street,
over cigarettes and whiskey

maggie submitted to Juniper Literary Journal

monday morning maggie's still here
sunday nights i'm her last date
always every sunday night,
every week
every month
it seems like forever
poets need a muse for release –
thought *she's in her sixties*, but at forty-four, looks
older; drugs, alcohol, and a rough life spent on the
streets, with a few years in a nevada brothel,
then five in prison aged her, now weak and weary,
youth's skills downgraded to now   whatever works –
her straggly hair and pendulous breasts
rests on my bed   while i dress and start breakfast for
us with toast, two eggs over easy, diced potatoes, and a
strong coffee roast gets both of us going, then she'll
leave me later with a kiss; sometimes she gets paid,
sometimes not, never know, i gave her a key in case she
needs a rest from life's test; after she leaves, i write in
poetry the stories she told me, most of them sad,
emotionally hard to deal with, then i down a beer with
a tear and start a new stanza

endings submitted to New Lines for publication

not a hotel, though they have rooms;
death waits in the emergency room
for me   for you   for everyone
who walks, wheels, or is carried in

healthy people don't go there for fun
no movies or theater happen here
only melodramas of pain and anguish

rooms are filled with prayers for health,
a priest constantly roams the halls
ready to give final absolution, no matter
if asked, it's a job that requires death;
the living have no need for it

only a call away, the undertaker waits,
ready to roll, pick up a client,
prepare for the final destination

toothpicks submitted to New Lines for publication

sit in a short
highball glass
on the edge of the maître d' desk
bunched together,
squeezed tight,
each one a clone
waiting to be picked
which one will win

we are no different
than any of them
we're all born bare-ass naked
boys and girls unsheathed
our destination not determined
like the small,
inconsequential toothpick
it has no choice
which lips it will part
only to be moistened and jabbed
between rows of gritty,
food-impacted teeth

as we mature
our lives delve into the
earthly grind of work and sorrow
with too few days of rest
to gather again
as we did at birth
naked and serene

a poet's life submitted to Juniper Literary Journal

after sunset
a table lamp is turned on
the poet finishes
another page in a notebook
then places it on top
of the pile of filled ones
on the floor near the door
next to his chair
where anyone who enters,
where anyone who dares,
needs to be careful
or they can slip or trip
over stacks of rhyme

at forty-nine he can write
a poem with bite
yet can't make a living
though his books sell well
because poetry's not a big sell
stanzas don't ring everyone's bell
what to do   what to do
after a few beers
rhyme time is over
at midnight, he starts a novel
and closes all the doors
to write about rich men,
and their street-wise wife whores
in hopes these books will sell
because he thinks
this feels like going to hell

he found himself in paradise

submitted to New Lines for publication

these last few days
no rush to leave
he searched for years to find her
this weekend never needs to end
though it will   come monday

how she escaped his grasp
while he searched for her
is one of the world's great mysteries
evolution can be explained
yet how he missed her   cannot

when together
he feels time has no value
tomorrow doesn't exist
heaven sent an angel
to bring him paradise on earth
though it is only temporary

like wind, she must blow away
to become a memory   and
he's only another client to her

king james submitted to New Lines for publication

the english christian bible
starts with this royal decree
the main book he endorsed
is meant for you and me

the holy rollers of today
are vehemently anti-gay
it's against their bible's way
to them, there is no sway

a bisexual king was he
slept with gentle men and a she
had many lovers   you will see
homosexuality   is for royalty

believers today won't sin in bed
back then, no one whispered or said
don't do that   unless you're wed
or the tower of london caught their head

pretty little girl

she is an active
five-year-old
smiles easily given
hugs too
most parents want a girl like her
she plays dress up with dolls
likes to run, skip, jump rope
started kindergarten last month

to her parents
she is their angel
dressed in pink
a cherished cherubic cupid
her future awaits

too young to be in pain
headaches bring tears
every week takes a train
to the big city   for radiation
the tumor's supposed to shrink
her autopsy form is in black ink

42nd street and broadway

area hotels, located
in prime midtown manhattan,
filled with tourists, busy business people,
who easily expense expenses
in the evening, after work, are like honey bees;
they pick out the pretty flowers
that walk and work on tenth-avenue
in bright, garish, translucent tops
with shear, tight, body-hugging leggings
and are drawn to their sweet pollen –
next day, city buses pass, belch fumes and smoke which
choke the masses
of straw-chewing scarecrows
who walk sidewalks mindlessly
going to and fro, then
return to somewhere in america
after they pollinate all night, guiltless,
and bear gifts for workers at home
never to mention illegal indiscretions
except on bowling night
after a few brews with the boys
while their wives never mention
the primal activities they too would,
while alone, twerk and tweak
for one enjoyable, satisfying week

whales are big mammals 1963

hippy culture, madras shirts, blue jeans
bad boys of song, rolling stones rule
pot outlawed, smoked anyway, every day
free love, free sex, no pay, except in experience

at sixteen, i was five-foot-ten, one-forty-five;
she was willing, at six foot one, all unshaved,
her naked body imposing, intimidating,
full, round breasts, fit, firm body, oh boy

my legs started to tremble, and
words fumbled,
mind went blank,
body went into automatic anticipation

not a first for me in high school
but now, i had second thoughts
possibly in over my head, literally, as she
approached and smothered me in her chest

i remember i left her house with my school books
exceptionally tired   and relieved   i survived
we met a few times again before summer break
luckily, my family traveled that year, i needed a respite

to recover

memory

we met in high school
same classes
same likes
same love
dated till marriage
children came
life was a love song
middle age grayed us
kisses never a fuss
still cared for each other
retirement plans stumbled a bit
had to downsize
but where to live
settled on adult care
lost most of my hair
bits of her memory did disappear
as did her ability to hear
she looks the same
her body didn't change
my love is still here
yet she isn't

poetic blueprint for insurrection

late at night, the woke awoke
poets meet in dark after work
while society retires

mirth and myth rise with words
whispers romp amongst the motley
who speak ill of the egotistical and
false prophets elected to serve and help

in the caverns of beer consumption
a literary resistance festers, with stanzas,
consonant rhymes to confuse and
amuse the literati   who look askance
at the nation's foibles and woes

while undereducated ignore books for looks
bravado for basic intelligence
to vote blindly for a convicted convict
who proudly proclaims to destroy the nation

jersey pine barrens

are empty of development
a few, old dilapidated buildings
are left from pre-banned
building codes

nothing there
but pitch pine trees
barely taller
than a man can reach up
take root in sandy soil
which somehow
finds its way into shoes
to irritate toes

the dirt roads
branch off the few paved ones
to leap deep into old-growth forest
where big city mobsters
occasionally visit
to bury their secrets
six feet down
in an unannounced
illegal desolate cemetery

enchanted dancers

the club's walnut-burled bar
in a dark area of the building
the elevated stage
awash in floodlights
reflect off polished chrome poles
the dancers use when working

they strut, gyrate, and move, until
the headliner finally appears
she only wears
a red paisley bandanna
customers throw money at her
as the tats on her ta-tas jiggle along
to the pounding, loud, high-decibel club music
conversations are minimized
except in the curtained private lounge
where purchased love ensues
and big, burly bouncers are only
a shout and two steps away
to make sure the girls are safe

and paid

sixty years later

already eighty
his mind never left viet-nam
vodka doesn't leave a scent
it dulls feelings, not memories
causes him to stumble and tumble
shrapnel in his left leg rises up
one after the other over the years
as the bumps disturb a deep sleep
unless blotted through bottles

raised in a home of faith and love
war changes some in different ways
it was not easy for him in the jungle,
constant tension from fear of ambush,
or a wrong step on a buried mine,
the hill he defended, attacked in
hand-to-hand combat with naked guerillas
who lunge at him with a bayonet
after he shot them dead
                    yet they still come at him
with drug-induced zombie soldiers

memories don't die easily
they need to be suppressed somehow
pills and booze usually do the trick–
the night table drawer holds a permanent cure
he knows it's against the law but

his wife hid the bullets

chaos in their lives

the children are hungry
while the fridge is full of lager
parents wash their clothes occasionally
bathe kids
    when they can't stand the stink
work to qualify for unemployment

only the beer is kept up to date
protective services tried to help
but never succeeded
when the children skip school
          for two weeks
police investigate
parents found in bed with a note
they left bags and bags of chocolate cookies for the kids
in death, they finally thought of them

maybe, someday

it's in the future
you know
non-committal
maybe, someday
that's how they weasel out
saying either yes or no

to be decided,
maybe, someday
when we get a chance
we will get around to it
maybe, someday

waiting

on your first date
you set day and time
then you had to wait
for your selection to show up
luckily, it went well
a first kiss led to more
as you said goodbye at the door

many meets later
marriage
a commitment for life
two children
a beagle and a cat
fill a happy home

a fateful day years later
a workday accident
hospice
funeral
finality

the *till death do us part*
commitment completed
a gold ring
      s l o w l y
slips off, and
life continues

alone

western cowboy melody

i want to sing a country song
of lost love and cowboy heartbreak
wild horses corralled and trained
like a tamed stallion saddled up to go

the open, unfenced green great plains
is where they ran and roamed
free from restraints and regulations
in the wild-west of memories

today, i'm hindered and hobbled
cities and highways tore up my way
there's no place to be free anymore
i feel penned in, can't open the door

stuck in civilization, my horse now a car
my barn's empty, stalls cobweb-filled
all i want to do is ride my way home
saddled up, and feel the air on my face

to ride high in a hand-tooled leather saddle
the up and down rhythm of a galloping mare
brings me closer to the filly my heart yearns for
a white-picket-fence where family can start

the dahmer cat

bitterly cold
winter weather's windless snow
falls gracefully
like lady lace delicately woven
it covers the landscape
as it drapes trees and lawns
in virgin white flakes
the moon reflects light when
i spot a feral feline feeding outside
by the wooden box i made for it
to shelter inside in bad weather

the morning milk i poured, it ate,
as is the cat kibble left last night,
as i always do, so it isn't hungry

the field mice are almost gone
from the nearby farmer's field
occasionally
i find body parts in my yard
to remind me
my semi-permanent cat
might be a serial killer

flowers

they are so delicate
precious petals pulsate
as a light northerly breeze blows in
beautiful banquets of color
shimmer in shades of blue, red, and yellow
all hues of the palette
cherished by many
a symbol of endured love
brings tears
to the heartbroken
as they're gently lowered
on a loved one's final resting place

klub kisses

the club's music
pounds out rhythms
as liquor flows
from bottles to lips
inhibitions masked
dance floor hands
explore gyrating bodies
where in usually private moments
two people love with intent
but now meaningless gropes, and
french kisses awash in beer
tangle in loveless mouths

tonight is tonight, and
tomorrow, not thought of
while restroom stalls
initiate intimacy
to be forgotten
with the morning sun;
hopefully,
with no surprises in months to come

smoke'n with willie nelson

never thought
i'd share her
in my old age
with willie at night

he lights up with me
and old mary jane
to bring back bong memories
he smoked for years

now, we share tales
of wasted youth
as old age pounces on us
with a deathly grip

it doesn't matter anymore
we chill out without a shout
just lay back in the sack
as she captures our minds

war zone

dirt, it's just dirt
a blood-soaked,
deadly,
disgusting dirt

wars are fought
over disputed dirt
there's enough to go around
for everyone

don't die over dirt
the killing must end
why not live on shared ground
in peace

all grown up

almost eighty, and
today i decided

i don't want to be an adult anymore

seventeen was a good age
no responsibilities
other than school,
have a good time dating,
do my homework,
show up for a part-time saturday job

today   i worry too much
   about adult children
    their marriages,
     their illnesses,
      their children, and
health as my body wore down after many years

too much of a burden
for an old mind to process
not as sharp as in youth
try to remember things
before they take flight
it's not easy
need to write them down quickly

i don't want to be an adult anymore

i'll live with it

that's all her text said to him
what did he give her, i wondered,
is it curable, regift-able, maybe both
can she return it when she wants

gifts, i found out, are varied
some take nine months to fruition
a few itch a lot on certain body parts
some are simple, sweet love whispers

the ones you're not crazy about
sometimes grow on you, like fungus,
stay for what seems like forever
but the best one is when he says *goodbye*

hope you can get over it
while you smile and think
i'll live with it

new england country store

rustic, dusty, wood beams overhead
open pickle barrels sit by the counter
wool shirts and plaid winter jackets hang
row after row in the rear room
as the musty smells of a century-old store
brings back barefoot memories of
ten-year-old boys
in summer months years ago
when my buddies and i swim
in fast-flowing creeks
in the middle of the densely treed mountains
as trout wiggle past
while we splash and float in the shallows
and sit on the muddy bottom
as ice-cold currents cool us
on a hot july day in vermont
while tall, old forest trees shade the
water and cause a slight breeze
to chill our young naked bodies; then
dress and walk back to the country store
to buy a sweet milk chocolate treat
and sit on the front steps
to enjoy the day's end before dinner

i long to be back

in colorado and wyoming
on the high plains
where wild horses
trample colorful wildflowers
under un-shoed hooves
tails float aimlessly
in thin mountain air
as they gracefully run
unhampered
free to roam
until government helicopters
spook them in a trap
then load magnificent, mighty steeds
onto trucks to be sold at auction
to meat-packing buyers
and selected restaurants

i park my car
in noisy, car-choked, urban new york, and
walk in a corner bodega at noon
to buy an ice-cold cola soda
on a hot july summer day
to wash down the city grit
stuck in my throat

unfolded future

last night
in a semi-sleep
the universe came to me
to unfold its darkest, deepest secret
a far future of nothing awaits
as in a permanent sleep
without pain or problems

blackness now known
it awakens my senses
enjoy today,
the smallest flower,
the smallest smile,
the rays of sunlight,
while i can
with every day
i stay awake

ba humbug

snow
belongs
on mountains
on barren fields
on far-away places
even out at sea
not on paved roads

while kids love
   snow angels and
   sledding down hills
it belongs to youth
not adults who shovel it
or drive on it

seniors forced indoors
imprisoned at home
sometimes solitary confinement

you know, new snow no go, for me
until i move somewhere warm
then a storm
can drop flakes
as much as it wants

retirement

every day is sunday
no job, no rush, sleep late
fill the days with doctors
  cardiologist
  pulmonologist
  dermatologist
  nephrologist
go to funerals of friends
until they're all buried and
none left

breakfast
lunch
dinner
watch the late news
midnight guest shows
   if i don't nod off

take a mary jane gummy before bed
sleep
wake up
start over

confessional

it hurts
it really hurts
venus took cupid's arrows and
violently stabbed at my broken heart
until it stopped beating out pheromones
when the girl i dated
decided to stray with her winter boyfriend

i was a mere summer dalliance

beauty distorted her personality
she was a national beauty contest finalist
how can anyone
be with a narcissist long-term

the reality
is to enjoy the roller coaster ride –
it will be short, exhilarating, and
memorable
never forgotten

from experience,
i guarantee it

forlorn

she sat next to me on a wooden bench
under a tall leafed oak tree in the park
her distinct perfume caught my attention
i couldn't help but notice her long hair
flowed down her voluptuous body
to drive my hormones into overdrive –
i spoke to her first, believe it or not,
one word led to another, and we kissed –
the affair of the heart was fulfilling
it lasted a few months until she
decided to return to her husband,
who, in all honesty, i did not know
even existed, until i asked for her hand
in marriage, then she told me,
with a passionate smooch, she had to leave,
to return to a life
left in haste years ago
when a midlife crisis hit, and
she ran from responsibility –
i sit on the bench every day, waiting,
hoping the love of my life will return

when a poet dies

they're brought into a library
and stuck in the poetry section
between arts and recreation books,
and geography and history texts,
according to the dewey decimal system
depending, of course
if the librarian likes your cover

otherwise

you're buried somewhere
in children's books
where they will drool and
wipe boogers all over you

ugh

lust

sometimes in life, you just know
although i am a modest person, and
my upbringing taught me manners –
what to say, when to say it,
to always be respectful of others

you are different, i can't help myself,
when i saw you, everything changed
i want to devour you completely,
to keep your naked body next to mine
forever

it is an instant deep love
i'm insanely attracted to you
your flame to my moth
i offer hesitancy
to the gods of lust and desire
as i have no need for it now, as
life wore me out   and
i'm tired

hospital emergency room

quick, on the table,
grab the tissues
the man on your left
has medical issues
he's blue, looks sick,
and an evangelical–
nurses tisk tisk
when he mentions a testicle

seems he made a vow
years ago of chastity;
never had sex,
only sprouted bombastity
said he'd only sleep with girls
if married, in bed,
or stay in it
when lifeless and dead

senior housing development magic show

    one day jim disappeared
he lived next door, but his heart stopped
    one day dave decided to leave, too
his wife went to make tea,
he left before she returned
    one day, nick, from across the street
left the block three years after his wife
    the 93-year-old man across from nick also left
he'd sit in the shade of his garage in the summer;
his nurse stayed till his kids came to close up
    the elderly couple three houses down, left
they kept wild raccoons in their attic,
never cleaned them out

    sadly, none of them came back in a black top hat
with a white rabbit under their arms
    their magic show has ended

balloons

there are two round ones
hanging over there
i'd like to play with them
but i do not dare

almost

we almost did it
summer of '63
in a rear rustic bungalow
up the hill near the top
too far and too steep
for my aunt or mother to ascend
crickets sing by the open window
surf city plays on my small transistor radio
set on the sill near our heads
we embrace
on an unmade twenty-year-old mattress
that today i would never even touch
let alone roll around naked on it much –
our kisses lit the match to start the fire
both of us ready to commit
when a breeze wafts in
loaded with pollen, and
she stood to search for allergy pills
her pocketbook torn asunder
she forgot them home
a moment of decision
to engage and ignore her discomfort
or drive her home

almost is now a dreaded word to me

forever next

yes
i admit you're another cut
on my king-size bedpost
where young princesses
of the realm are entertained,
sometimes days at a time

they are in the past –
i wandered about
to look for what i thought was love

in a search for my queen
i discovered intimacy
is not caring
but only carousing
while being caressed

if it soothes your mind
you are my forever
you are my last notch

poison ivy

it looks innocent enough
green leaves entice
asks to be touched or
brushed against in passing

similar to a bad relationship
seems harmless at first
then becomes an irritant, and you
try to rid yourself of it

as you continue life
you'll never forget
this personal experience
was an exasperating time

suddenly, the realization
it's not an easy thing to do;
you had to live with it
for a while until it's gone

information science hypotheses

reality is not really reality
our lives are not the real deal
but an advanced computer program
the same as our computer play games
with almost sentient abilities

god is ones and zeros
where there is no universal order
since no one on earth built the program
our sensibilities are built on gigabytes
the question is
what happens
when the supercomputer turns off

orange tabby

the winter storm is almost near
northern arctic winds barrel in
tree's limbs shiver from numbing cold,
summer leaves are but a memory
an empty bird's nest built in july
wedged between two twigs up high
fights to remain as bits blow off
finally, its attempt to remain is nigh
i sit in my home reading a book
as my windows rattle and quiver
a cat curls up by my rear glass door
raises its head to give me a look
my knife cuts up some chicken slivers
then pour milk into a small crystal bowl
and open the door to let it in –
at a regal gait, it decides to enter
a hungry feline graces my home
to finish the food i serve on the floor
on my wife's bone china plate –
the milk it slurped and meat it ate
raindrops grew into a torrential flood
my guest jumped up to sit on my lap
a rounded fur ball soon fell asleep
no longer alone, a friend i will keep

windows

in manhattan,
skyscrapers touch clouds
residential buildings are
extremely high
residents rarely use
shades or curtains
sunlight floods
all rooms with an airy feel

each window tells a story
behind the panes
the widow cries
after her soulmate dies,
children
who miss a living parent,
an elderly sickly spinster
alone in the city

in other buildings,
someone has a telescope
a viewer's bonanza
of spy activity   to see
lovers loving, some,
with others joining in;
life lived both ordinary and not

each glass a door
to someone's life
a veritable smorgasbord
of titillating tales
some with bland views,
mostly boring and dull
yet a voyeur watches expectantly
for sensuality

how do you say goodbye

when you know
there's no tomorrow
no pills are working
dawn's sunshine won't warm everyone
or announce a new day starts, as
tonight's slumber is for all
permanent for few–
to let go of a hand wet with shed tears
while the religious mumble final prayers
loud as a whisper
only select ears can hear
life is always terminal
it's fatal for all

if hearts are filled with love
how do you say goodbye

louisa of east 8th street, off 2nd avenue, n.y.c.

she wears a small, tight-fitting mini-cotton dress of
colorful bitsy florals; five inches above the left knee i
see on her inner thigh tiny pink cat tats, while the
bouncy braless chest on her young petite body waves to
me with each step– the thin, one-inch track marks on
her forearm almost gone now; when she smiles, most of
her teeth are still there because a friendly dentist to the
stars fixed them in exchange for drugs, intimate favors
on wednesdays after hours, before treatments– it's been
a whirlwind attraction since we met in washington
square after a civil rights protest; it was overcrowded,
we bumped into each other, our eyes locked, desires ran
rampant, breathing optional, all i wanted was to devour
her forever, totally, in my apartment, on the art deco
metal bed i found on the sidewalk, and a hard foam
mattress i bought second hand in an uptown harlem
church's thrift shop– i grab the solid cast iron bars on
the roller-coaster, lock it down firmly, then hold on
tight as the ride to heaven begins; we are buckled in
securely with no space between us, as we experience
the swish and dips of an exciting amusement, until the
chinese take-out delivery boy rings the doorbell with
our dinner of shrimp fried rice, two egg rolls, very dark
hot and sour soup, with pieces of pork, tofu,
mushrooms, and bamboo shoots, as cut-up scallions
float on top

wisdom of king solomon

her husband is a steak and potato type guy
home at six, demands dinner ready
a handy guy at work, too handy at home
makeup hides   black and blue bruises
always stops at the tavern after work
a few too many down the hatch
comes home an angry drunk
a small man in a big world
a raging bull is hard to stop
a kitchen cleaver does the trick
slice and dice, then bring to a boil
cooked meat will never spoil

problem solved

nerdy, dirty, and flirty girls

with their chrome round wire-rimmed glasses,
long skirts, braless blue butterfly tattooed breasts
poking through tight washed and shrunken tee shirts,
waist-length brunette ponytails, a nose ring, tongue
pierced, arms sleeved, with liberal libidos and can
speak of ferlinghetti, ginsberg, or hirschman; they are
my bread-and-butter girls

yet, like a gourmet meal, i'd like to try the other items
on the menu, such as cheerleaders who are like
bubblegum bubbles and would never date me, with
their blond hair, blue eyes, short skirts, and tight
sweaters as they hang on the arm of the school's
quarterback while they listen to the current day's
singers instead of reading a book with words put
together in strings of sentences

yes, i'd like to drop my toes in that water occasionally
to swim around a bit, and like diet beer, i'm told it's not
that fulfilling, though it does taste good at first

cruel summer

this was my first date with her
never expected she'd go out with me,
she was gorgeous,
but i asked anyway; she said yes–
recently received my driver's license,
nervous to drive mom's car, my date asked to go to the
nude beach at sandy hook –
do you cook she asked as i drove
    sometimes, but not a lot
she took my right hand off the wheel
placed it down there
    where i'd never been before

beads of sweat formed on my forehead
the car swerved, tried to regain control
of both my car and my emotions
when in a low, throaty voice, she whispered
    stir the mashed potatoes a little faster
my foot went numb
the car veered off the road
stopped in front of a fire hydrant –
    finally, potatoes mashed
we continued, parked, and walked
to the beach

she threw a blanket down, undressed,
then started to sun herself;
i stood mesmerized, dressed, and stared
while everyone else, naked, had a great time –
although afterward, i called a few times
this was the only date we had

i decided at seventeen
maybe i'd like a cooking class

observations

i saw her in the market yesterday
in the pasta aisle
in front of the long spaghetti boxes
with her long, never-ending legs
she stretched to bend down to a low shelf –
i remember rumors my girlfriend heard
at the beauty parlor last week
what the beautician said about this woman,
who's muscular and extremely shapely,
is a masseuse who massages
like a cat cleans itself,
while her mousey husband,
emaciatingly thin with horn-rimmed glasses,
a deep blue bowtie on a white starched shirt,
stands behind her in the market and
watches her place brown boxes in her cart –
male shoppers pass
stare till their eyes fall out
as she raises her hands overhead
to reach a top shelf,
grabs two large cans of tomato sauce
with onions, basil, and italian spices
to jam next to premade pork and beef meatballs
taken from the butcher section
into her cart before checking out

winter

a december snow storm   arrives
slashes and slides   into the calm
as wild weather predictions   hold true

flurries fall fast   begin to stack
empty beaches   now colored white
westerly winds   a furious force

opaqueness hides   rollicking ocean waves
summer sand flies   nowhere to be seen
seagulls shelter together   on a concrete parking lot

hotdog vendors bake   in sunny southern climes
boardwalk amusement rides   deathly still
blustery carnival music   a warm june memory

months to go   till summer springs back to life
silence contrasts   with missing cantankerous crowds
this is winter   at the jersey shore

emotions

hard to express
what's in your heart
if the other person
walks away

goes somewhere
    anyplace   but here
gone from your life
someone you held dear

left for good, they set sail
i'll continue to look
till i'm long dead, and
my body's cold and pale

this is true teenage love
always present in your mind
until sixty years later
you read of their passing

summer storm

walls of water
torrentially fall without stop
as my clock tires
from counting too many hours

the hardest earth
can no longer support
its own weight, while
earthworms float up to survive

soft brown mush absorbs and
covers the shoes it covets
as it tries to hold them forever
like a breakup's grasp at lost hearts

birds fly overhead
to laugh at the shoeless
who lost something dear
in a garden of mud

january storm

virgin white flakes
embrace all they touch,
its brightness
blinds the sightful,
enthralls the young, and
wearies waiting shovels
which stand still in the garage
next to the ice melt salt
before they can begin
to kiss the snow

florist shop.

at seventeen
i was shoulder to shoulder
in society's garden of women
with roses, lilies, bright daisies,
and the always present daffy daffodils
all within reach of my jacket lapel
where i could walk proudly with one
and friends would wonder
how i plucked it from the group

now, i tell them
pretty petals are not attracted
to a more handsome vase or suit,
my secret is
i smile sunlight on them

east 21street memory

in my youth
the elderly, six-foot-tall, zoftig lady
who lived across the street
always walked her hotdog dog
every morning, while dressed in her finest
sheer white nightgown and gold slippers, she
never bent down
to pick-up after friedrich did his business
on her front lawn, while the
spanish kid who mowed on thursdays
unknowingly trampled it into the soil
to help fertilize the lush, tall green grass
while i rode my bike up and down
the streets of brooklyn
cars and trucks ignored
because youth has a protective shield
of innocence and ignorance
to never think of death or injury

job justification

thousands of pages mailed out
tons of black ink used
information to be shared by all
except for one low-level employee

who is a special h.r. hire
paid well for no talent
or work experience
yet given a manual function

he is the blank page stamper
this page is intentionally left blank
in bold, black typeface
inserted in every mailer

freedom

almost midnight, the moon's very bright
a flick of the wrist turns off all the lights
as on cat's puffy pads, she sneaks out the door
certain, she'll suffer abuse no more

she leaves for freedom to regain her rights
marriage vows in tatters, tonight, no more fright
no more pushes or shoves, with yells and screams
a special sugar added to his tea when it steams

all pictures burned, and none will be found
his chopped-up parts buried six feet underground
deep in the woods in a field miles away
a miserable man no longer holds sway

name and hair color, she decides to change
single, frisky, ready, to date on the range
no family or friends to worry about now
on fields of men she intends to plow

reflections of an old man

in old age
i now have respect
for the never-ending blackness
at life's end
no matter how small a creature
or religious a person
it's all the same

although, as a young boy
it never crossed my mind
when i found a huge ant hill and
blew it up with firecrackers
like a volcanic eruption
to try to kill the bugs

i understand now
the life store we all live in
is only open
a set number of hours
    then closes
and all the accumulated things
stored in it are gone
wasted
lost forever
permanently

agog

bob was agog
when they met
her beauty breathtaking
she was agog at bob's agog
because she never enjoyed
being agog before this agog
and vowed
not to be agog again
poor agog bob

on a city street

on an early morning walk,
i pass a doorman's door;
across the street
is a project for the poor
a shiny rolls-royce
stops close to me and
a woman steps out
with diamonds for all to see
she passes a tradeswoman
who walks the street
and the homeless man
who by the curb is asleep

with indifference
she ignores the city's sheep
who roam around
unnoticed, unbound, yet
call city sidewalks
their only home

if we ever meet

i'd tell you
i see you
     don't hide behind a *no*
feelings betray, and your glow
blinds me
i'm a bear to your honey
irresistible
sweetness overflows from your heart
i'm meant for you
don't
     walk away
it's been a long time

i looked for love
finally found you

i had to slow my search
to notice you
overlooked too quickly by zeal

if we ever meet
i'll hold on to you
forever

as an old man

i relish the simpler pleasures
   to sit on a bench by the sea
   hear waves thrown upon a beach
   the sweet smell of salt air as it wafts in
where children splash and giggle
at the same sandy place
my parents brought me when
i was young and impish

mom placed
a heavy wool blanket on the sand
stretched it out
to be our picnic table
where the woven basket was placed on a corner
and iced, canned salmon sandwiches
on white bread served to us
with its small bones, i had to pick out

to this day,
i hate salmon sandwiches
and mildly cool water
poured from a plaid thermos
to drink on a scorching hot day

i just want to sit here by myself
to relish memories of family long gone

unseen and unnoticed

they are secret lovers
hidden from prying eyes
   although
as they spoke in front of others
often   with words of care and concern

yet they never uttered
the three syllables
lovers say
when together

they never meet
except online
separated by continents,
time zones,
and in front of a dozen people
in a live group chat

theirs, a hidden relationship
unfolded for all to see
yet unnoticed
except by them

sanctuary seclusion and quietude

silence
deathly quiet
alone   a recluse

in his locked cell
the monk renounces society
chooses solitary study

pages of gospel
echo in his soul
spill silently

onto moving lips
until the awaited never-ending bliss
finally arrives

never-ending love

it's been a long time
since she was with her husband –
after their marriage at eighteen
he was drafted and
six months later sent to war
never to return

he was killed
buried overseas
alone, she never remarried
he was the love of her life

now, in old age
never experienced children
or grandchildren
as she sits in her white,
doily-covered lounge chair
    reads
or quietly stares out the window
at   nothing   in   particular
to wait patiently
until she can be with him again

her heart pierced

the question arose
could she ever return
to the person she was
after a trusted love
couldn't be trusted

cheated on
he lied they'd be together
build a forever life of love
with snuggles and cuddles
on getaway weekends
all the right words
play to a lovelorn heart

until the phone call
one night
a significant other
found her
on social media

they spoke for hours
two devastated lovers
two would be *forevers*
two tormented souls

now fast friends
in misery
        forever

rubino ristorante cucina italiano

she finally said yes to a date
we met at half past eight
i order rollatini on a large plate
the waitress brought eggplant for eight
i eat one, serve another to my date

six are left to cut and eat
red sauce stains i must be neat
take two more on my plate
she took three, which she ate
one remains, drowns in marinara
finished, she stands, says sayonara
no hug or goodnight kiss goodbye
my night ends with a troubling sigh
took the last one home for my treat
put in a pot, then turn up the heat

she was nice, but felt like ice
i called to ask her out again, twice
she decided there would be no thrice
now out of my system, i lost the itch
i don't want to be
with a cold-hearted bitch

why

yellow sun bright in the sky
clouds of white aimlessly float by
why all i see is darkness in life
there is no tomorrow

and i don't know why

pushers, pimps, prostitutes

manhattan's underbelly of sordidity
repulsive to those upright and proper
who wallow in distaste and tisk tisks
until darkness covers their foibles
hidden from society in:
empty board rooms
dark hallways
private spaces
shaded from the sunlight of exposure
when they join in
sinful, shameful, sexualities
no different
then the ones they whisper about

bones

old bones
creak, crack, break
calcium deprived
plaster casts feeble activity
mentally young
they long to bounce on young bones again
like ships that pass in the night
they never bump into each other
as they did years ago
as they did in their youth
as they try to remember
as they try to remember

late night meeting

before midnight
television off
readied for bed
when i heard
bukowsky call out to me
how about another beer
don't be afraid, come near,
i liked your poem
about the woman who shopped naked
in her six-inch red-soled stilettos

overjoyed he enjoyed my poetry
i overlooked the fact
she wore sandals, not high heels,
a straw hat, and a thin gold chain belt
plus, he offered me a cigarette and
we smoked, talked, and drank for hours

next day i told my analyst
about the poet i spoke to last night
he was perturbed
      my ghost got it wrong
invalidating my subconscious thoughts
and added to my insecurities
plus, i don't drink liquor or smoke

nobody notices nina

people float in waves of humanity
in manhattan's times square
while she squats by the curb
on flattened cardboard boxes, and
    loudly hawk's pocketbooks
    in a distinctive foreign accent

they are maybe leather
maybe brass accents
maybe impressive designer labels
at steep discounts
from duplicate, expensive,
fifth avenue luxury retail stores
as police stroll by and
ignore her
intent on keeping painted bare-breasted ladies
who are available for pictures with tourists
in the designated spaces
provided for street performers

costco

they line up
   to wait
   to rush
when store doors open

people jostle and jumble
tussle and bumble
to wait for free food samples
especially   at lunchtime

a lady in front starts to push
my eyes are glued
   to her spandex tush
a big round blob
of jelly roll smoosh

i buy what i need
and plenty i don't
from a year's worth of ketchup
to a lifetime supply
of cheddar cheese dips

the warehouse walk
is basically a product stalk
and at the end of the hike
i sit silently and sing a song

and eat a dollar-fifty drink
with a one-foot-long

black

they don't matter in flint michigan
undrinkable water saves money
the white state government is deaf
it's only a depressed black city

in europe the oppressed left
came to america to prosper
where are these detroitians to go

the water in georgia is clean
they can drink all they want
if they don't get railroaded
into a prison farm chain gang

in mississippi
where they bypass
the courts and lynch
from the nearest tree

except for skin color,
this can be you or me
in a country
that's the land of the free

maybe

brill building 1966

the fifth-floor office faces times square
seated by a back corner
is a cool cat with shoulder-length hair,
white, torn tee shirt, untrimmed short beard
with a melodic musical gift –
his songs float from the soundboard
with big-name singers eager
to record soon-to-be hit tunes –
a rolled cigarette with pungent smoke
dangles from his lips
grey ash sprinkles over yellowed ivory keys,
as the young girl from texas,
stands behind him, her voice
strong, throaty, vibrant, fills the room
between swigs of kentucky bourbon
while old, white men record producers,
sit around, think how they can sign her
until they find she lives with the piano player
who discovered her singing
in a run-down, dark, dank biker bar in fort worth
and owns her   contract

an arrangement

she made a commitment
although no one would blame her
if she walks away,
his mind water-logged and
statements nonsensical,
yet she couldn't, and refused
to warehouse a much older husband,
the father of her children, and
when she indulged in affairs of the heart
to satisfy primal urges with special girlfriends
he was the person she returned to –
he was her security blanket, and
his blindness of her carnality
due to age and impotence
increased her sense of duty to him
in sickness and in health

maybe a letter from lord byron

the french sun in summer pales
compared to the young,
brightest beach bodies
whilst i play there with them
in romps of gentility until dusk
their affection for spirits from grapes
never seems to end
as i then am forced to endure
uninhibited female charms
as a young man is required to do
when a lady of the realm
requests your attention –
last night in blackness
her knight wandered halls and hills
to call for her
unbeknownst
she was encamped behind a guest's door
being thoroughly relished, and
tomorrow, her amour leaves for home
where the trip will be long and weary
only the thought
of your warmth under the shining stars
embraced with me in bliss
makes the journey back to you worthwhile

love is in the arena

football is a brutal sport
injuries abound all around
players leave mid-game
in each game permanence lives
someone is a star
someone is to blame

in the super-bowl yesterday
love was *swiftly* shown
    in the stands and
    on the jumbo screen
when it was over
    on the field
a bearded victor
kissed his fair maiden
amidst mayhem of celebration
before a trophy was presented
in the quick marriage capital
called las vegas

simple joy

delicately hold a small wildflower
with two fingers
watch the vivid purple-blue petals
while they shimmy
from your breath
its symmetry mesmerizes
as the world shrinks
in your sight
obliterates everything
only the simple joy
in your fingers
   now count

magical kiss

a kiss always buries hate
skin color disappears
political views submerge
religious beliefs vanish
bigotry and racism gone
give a kiss, get a kiss
it's hard to hate
          when you kiss

strong trees

mighty oaks stand tall and straight
one of the strongest woods around
with roots dug deep in the ground

down the road is a sweet maple tree
with tight fibers and slow-tapped juice
once cooked, is bottled for you and me

a hickory tree rounds out the batch
all three, when cut will finally match
when stripped of bark and splintered down

they all become short with pointed tips
to be a toothpick between my lips

enough

she walks away silently,
deaf to his pleas for forgiveness
her wounded pride
motivation
for a life-changing move
her self-respect
assaulted too long
finally, packs and leaves
for the airport
with no clear destination
except it has to be warm,
far away from him, where
he would never guess
to start a new life
the ticket agent said the next flight out
was to new mexico,
she took it, and flew away
to the enchanted land
of taos and santa fe
she joins a writer's commune
writes her novel
smokes piayu for inspiration
when she meets her soulmate
changed her name to hers
shaved both sides of her head
attached beads to her braids and
lives a peaceful, quiet life of love

my kisses

can you feel them
mental kisses
on your sweet cheeks
thoughts by scent
sent by thoughts
across many miles and byways
over distant hills

i dream of you in my arms
never to let go
your smiles resonate in memory
only to be real
when i dream

broken dream

high school athlete
a football star
girls crush on him
college scouts beg for him
university enables fame
sets collegiate records
drafted into the pros
a major league player
fortune thrown at him
in third year injured
doctors say it will be a miracle
if he can ever run again
after two years of therapy
he can now walk with a cane,
what about his tomorrow career
he feels like a car
with a powerful engine
                  ready to race
but one tire is flat
full of potential
yet hampered

lollipop girls[1]

when in england
see them stand
in rain, snow, sleet and fog
with a smile and a wave
they're always there
some are tall
some quite small
then there are the ones
so full and round
they're jolly good
to be around
the tiny, thin ones
can be blown away
if the wind is strong one day
don't ever try and
kiss a lollipop girl
if you get frisky
she'll shout out
STOP!

---

[1] Crossing guards are called lollipop girls

relationship

on their first date together
day and time set
then had to wait
for her selection to show up
luckily, it went well
first kiss led to more
as he said goodbye at the door

many meets later, marriage
a commitment for life
two children and happy times
until a fateful day seven years later
a workday accident
   hospital
      hospice
         funeral
           finality
till death do us part
a gold ring slowly slips off, and
life continues
                alone
again

almost

we almost did it
summer evening of '63
in a rental rear rustic bungalow
up the hill near the top
almost too far and steep
for my aunt or mother to ascend
crickets sing by the open window
surf city plays on my a.m. radio
set on the sill near our heads
we embrace
on an unmade twenty-year-old mattress
that today i would never even touch
our kisses lit the match to start the fire
both of us ready to commit, almost,
as a breeze wafts in
loaded with pollen
she stood to search for allergy pills
her pocketbook torn apart
forgot them home
a moment of decision
either engage and ignore her discomfort
or drive her home

almost is a dreaded word to me

love question

if we spend tonight together
will it be love or lust

fruition or frustration
can our lives together

be soft as passionate kisses
or a sunburn

where tanning is pleasant
but ends up red and burnt

if we spend the night together
will it be forever or forgotten

a recurring nightly dream
or a recurring nightmare

guess the only way to find out
is if we spend tonight together

backstabbed

the eagle left its nest
for a mere moment
and the black crow
flew in, ate the eggs,
with one eye to the sky
to spy for its return
to the nest of its unwilling host
and escape its wrath

nine minutes away
be home soon
his unexpected text read
    she *panicked*
both need to get dressed
    immediately
make the bed   make her face
spritz perfume around the room
push him out   lock the door
different men fill her needs
ten years of marriage unravel
her wants neglected   due to his meds
she has special friends visit
with no emotional feelings
except for lust and release

broken eggs can't be repaired
only replaced

helplessness

the grass in the yard
was mowed yesterday
its growth sheared short
cuttings removed,
reminds me
of her final day in hospice

i can't see
her beauty anymore
or relish a sterling quick wit
the sky's as pale as my emotions
don't know her final words
or final thoughts
the induced coma to eliminate pain
stole those moments
i will wander through life
missing her, and
speak to a granite monument
instead of at night
her warm body
next to mine

stamps

licking is quicker
sticking is sticky
your body
my envelope

rosaline

unforgiven
not forgotten
some things are heartbreakers
a person can't live with

when you give your love
   totally
    without hesitation
     vows taken for life
      broken in secret
       until discovered
life seems meaningless
when friends betray
become hidden lovers

brutus lives
the pain unbearable
no matter
how many sunrises shine bright
or new loves arrive
the river styx beckons

a girl called sparkle

daisies and daffodils
spring up every year
hemmed in
by violet and blue wildflowers
bunched tightly together
on the lined green fields
where she stays forever
her wild ride of life over
sparkle rode it with abandon
without a care for herself
while the pleasures of sin
took a toll
on her body and soul
until her twilight
crashed one fateful night
in a dark, curtained back room
of a seaside dance club called doom
with a patron
who violently stopped her ride
her lifeforce left
with the morning tide

play the apollo in harlem

nerves raw
glittery gold lamé sparkles on some
on amateur night   sweat, stains shirts
she stands alone in the wings and waits
while the guy ahead of her walks on
rubs the stump   then's center stage
one joke after the other, he
                        bombs
                badly—
            boos
resonate and echo back and forth
music starts, the hook comes out, he's gone
    next
hesitant   one foot before the other   she walks out
rubs the stump   then's center stage
she's young, in teens, torn jeans, worn-out sleeves
it's her sunday best when you're in state care

silence reigns, anticipation rules
the band plays, and singing starts
clear, crisp, concise, strong melodious voice
the audience roars approval
a brushed-out afro frames a tiny face
with a foot-wide smile   she's a hit
wins an invitation to come back next week
then leaves
to return to a brooklyn foster home
where life, as usual, continues

dissection of the republican political party

time to cut out the gangrene
rid the nation of its cancer
pour bleach on open wounds
wipe away political puss
foul thinkers only want power
the benefits of prestige hidden
from the misguided, under-educated
who vote against their interests
time after time after time
until they are impoverished, and
die from lack of proper healthcare

whispers

usually, nobody speaks of their prejudices publicly
they talk softly and only to those who are close
doesn't matter the subject or theme of hate
nothing is off limits to unacknowledged bigots

black, white, red, yellow, or rainbow mixed
unspeakable nicknames, thought quietly
rarely shouted to declare one's uncouth intention
they sneak about silently and hiddenly obstruct

tear off the bandage, pull out the surrounding hair
whisper no more; shout out; *they are there*
let the world know how you want to scare
don't hide from scorn, it's you i dare

trans ocean flight

row 18, seat:
a   middle-aged woman reads a novel of a hovel
b   teenager games a drone on a cell phone
c   broker circles a kernel in the wall street journal
d   young bride awaits her honeymoon ride
e   groom sits anxiously at her side
f   window seat empty

halfway through the flight, the captain announces
please stay in your seats and buckle your seatbelts
there is an unexpected fuel loss
we should arrive on time, though

    the middle-aged woman puts her book down
starts to cross herself, and white knuckles the armrest
    the teen's calm, his earplugs in, volume high,
concentration on the game
      broker texts goodbye, with a sigh, to his wife
      the bride starts to tremble and cry, too young to die
      hubby tries to calm his wife, too stressful with strife

the plane is in final approach to land
flaps are down, airspeed reduced, airport ahead
as the flight descends shudders and shakes
people scream, some tuck their heads
almost down,
then....

spanish flu
   a sonnet

my fever rises when i see you
your robust figure can capture
hearts and minds in morning dew
to love you all day in heartfelt rapture

a love so full it can burst and fracture
with lips pursed and full of kisses
can't wait to make you my darling mrs
on a pedestal high up to admire with stature

but you ignore my gesture
and deny my intense desires
why is my love so much lesser
your mind is now full from useless liars

why won't you even stop and talk
but it is only you i want to stalk

lottery

usually, winner takes all
sometimes there are splitzies
normally big lottery paydays
are a zero-sum game
sudden death to millions of players
after each nightly draw

death by inches for low payouts
two bucks, four, sometimes hundreds
but the losing paper ticket is useless
dreams destroyed
hopes vanquished
retirement delayed
billion-dollar payout paid
winner kept secret forever,
except to accountants and lawyers
who help mitigate taxes
while you and i
are back on the treadmill of life

two are too many

if one wife's not enough
polygamy's the answer
sometimes it can be tough
two wives are definitely rough

hospital

he walks into the hospital
when the angel of death
steps directly behind
to take his last breath
then the undertaker
wheels him out
zippered in a large, black plastic bag
to whisk away on an overcast day

the widow is bereft of compassion
for doctors who negligently killed him
then tried to cover up their oops, we goofed–
insurance paid off
with a sizable check
as she basks in acapulco sun,
drinking pina coladas on the beach
while her new, young local boyfriend
flexes tightly toned body
in a barely-there string thong
to amuse
his american sugar momma

to create a poem

quietness is exquisite and desired
while i sit in the park
on a bench
under a large shade tree
as it cools and comforts me
with eyes closed to enjoy a breeze
my mind free-floats
words are easy to put in a line
then two
when a young man
asks *can i speak to you*

no   please don't
can't you see i'm working

Thank you for reading my poetry.

For more of my books
please check out my website

www.CreativeFiction.net

on **Instagram** lookup
elliot_m_rubin
people poems

www.ingramcontent.com/pod-product-compliance
Lightning Source LLC
Chambersburg PA
CBHW071327130626
46556CB00004B/1790